ESMERALDA A. MARTINEZ

3 DE JULIO DE 1995

BEHIND THE NEWS

VIOLENCE
AGAINST WOMEN

INTERNATIONAL WOMEN'S DAY

MILLION
W MEN
RISE

MILLIONWOMENRISE.COM

Emma Marriott

WALTHAM FOREST LIBRARIES

904 000 00495956

Published in 2017 by Wayland
Copyright © Hodder and Stoughton 2017

Wayland
Carmelite House, 50 Victoria Embankment
London, ECY4 0DZ

All Rights Reserved.
Produced for Wayland by Tall Tree Ltd
Editors: Emma Marriott and Jon Richards
Designer: Malcolm Parchment

ISBN 978 1 5263 0512 1
E-book ISBN 978 0 7502 8819 4

Dewey number: 303.8'8'082-dc23

10 9 8 7 6 5 4 3 2 1

Printed in China

Wayland is a division of Hachette Children's
Group, an Hachette UK company
www.hachette.co.uk

The publisher would would like to thank the following
for their kind permission to reproduce their photographs:

Shutterstock.com unless stated otherwise:
Front cover: Paul Lurrie, Sadik Gulec, Tatiana Belova
John Gomez (4 – posed by model), Paul Lurrie (5),
Wiki_Commons (6), Wiki_Commons (7), Dan
Kosmayer (8 – posed by model), Baevskiy Dmitry (9),
Wiki_Commons (10), Getty Images (11), Monkey
Business Images (12 – posed by models), © Ole Spata/
dpa/Corbis (13), © Bill Nation/Sygma/Corbis (14),
Wiki_Commons (15), Wiki_Commons (16), Wiki_
Commons (17), Wiki_Commons (18), © Stephen
Barnes/Demotix/Corbis (19), Wiki_Commons (20), REX/
Photonews Service Ltd (21), JStone (22), Wiki_Commons
(23), Wiki_Commons (24), Zurijeta (25 – posed by model),
Val Thoermer (25 – posed by models), Wiki_Commons
(26), Suzanne Tucker (27), Wiki_Commons (28),
© Hkrunning/Dreamstime.com (29), TonyV3112 (29),
MCP/REX (30), © Mike Kemp/In Pictures/Corbis (31),
Wiki_Commons (32), © Annibale Greco/Corbis (33),
© Annibale Greco/Corbis (34), Wiki_Commons (35),
Wiki_Commons (37), Wiki_Commons (37), © Zou
Zheng/Xinhua Press/Corbis (38), ChameleonsEye
(38), gary yim (39), Wiki_Commons (39), © MONEY
SHARMA/epa/Corbis (41), RAFP/Getty Images (41),
Wiki_Commons (41), © Alex Masi/Corbis (42),
Wiki_Commons (43), Olga Rosi (44 – posed by model),
Wiki_Commons (45).

CONTENTS

A VIOLATION OF HUMAN RIGHTS

Every week, the news brings us stories of violence against women. From domestic abuse and rape to forced abortions, female genital mutilation (FGM) to murder, all are shocking examples of violence affecting women, devastating lives across the globe and within every level of society.

What is violence against women?

Violence against women can take many forms – physical, sexual and psychological. It can include overt acts of violence, such as murder and rape, as well as more hidden forms of abuse, such as forced marriage and the trafficking of women into prostitution or servitude.

The most common form of violence happens within a marriage or partnership, and women and girls of all ages can fall victim to it. It can happen at home, at school, within the general community and can even be perpetrated by those in authority.

Many organisations across the world are working to combat violence against women and it is increasingly recognised as a violation of human rights and a public health issue. The United Nations has pledged, under its UNITE campaign launched in 2008, to raise public awareness

Many female victims experience violence in their own homes at the hands of people they know, including husbands, fathers and brothers.

and political will in order to prevent all forms of violence against women and girls wherever they may live.

So many questions

Our immediate reaction is why does this still happen to so many women across the world? Who are the likely victims and what effect does it have? How can we stop it happening? And how does the media portray violence against women? Does the majority of abuse go unreported? In this book we go behind and beyond the news in an attempt to answer some of these difficult questions.

These women are taking part in a flash mob dance in Washington Square Park, New York City, USA, in 2013. It was organised by 'One Billion Rising', a group that campaigns around the world against the rise in violence against women.

'At least one in every three women globally has been beaten, coerced into sex or otherwise abused in her lifetime, with rates reaching 70 per cent in some countries.'

United Nations Development Fund for Women.

THE LONGER VIEW

Violence against women has a long history, reflecting deeply embedded beliefs about the inferiority of women, and has been used as a means of power and control. The extent of violence has always been difficult to measure as, even today, the vast majority of abuse is not reported by the victims.

Conflict

Sexual violence has often been seen as an inevitable accompaniment to war. Armies of the ancient Greek, Persian and Roman Empires, as well as soldiers of the Napoleonic era, were known to rape.

A global summit – End Sexual Violence in Conflict – was held in London in June 2014, co-chaired by former British Foreign Secretary William Hague along with UN Special Envoy, actress Angelina Jolie.

• *During World War II, girls and women were sexually enslaved by the Japanese army and German women were subject to mass rape by advancing Soviet soldiers.*

• *In the Bosnian War (1992–1995), rape was used as a means of ethnic cleansing predominantly by Serbian soldiers targeting Bosnian women and girls. In 1994, in the eastern African state of Rwanda, rape was similarly used as a means of genocide, with women being intentionally impregnated by HIV-infected men.*

• *In response to this, international communities began to recognise rape as a weapon of war. In 2008, the UN*

This Russian poster urges the audience to 'open your eyes' – to the domestic abuse of women and girls.

Security Council affirmed that 'rape and other forms of sexual violence can constitute war crimes, crimes against humanity or a constitutive act with respect to genocide'.

Domestic violence

Within marriage, the law has been slow to criminalise sexual assault as it was widely believed that a woman surrendered her consent when she married. In the early 1800s, most legal systems accepted wife-beating as a husband's right. By the end of the 19th century, most Western courts denied that a husband had a right to chastise his wife, but few women had realistic sources of help.

• *Since the 1970s, many changes have occurred in the public perception of sexual assault, partly as a result of the feminist movement, which brought the issue of domestic violence into the open, campaigning for the police to treat domestic violence in the same manner as any other assault.*

• *While domestic violence is generally outlawed in the Western world, it is viewed differently in other countries where husbands and wives are not considered equals.*

• *Globally, nearly half of 15- to 19-year-olds think a husband is justified in beating his wife under certain circumstances.*

WHO AND WHY?

Who are the perpetrators of violence against women and are certain women more likely to experience abuse? Who are the ones at greatest risk? Why does it happen and what are the factors that cause it?

Women of all ages

Violence, whether it is in the home, at school or further afield, affects women and girls of all ages across the globe and within all sectors of society. It is caused by a host of factors, from cultural and religious beliefs to economic pressures, marital breakdowns, previous exposure to violence and warfare.

The victims

While violence affects on average 35 per cent of women globally, there are regions of the world where women are much

Many victims of abuse feel isolated and alone because they believe that the law and those around them will not protect them from further violence.

Easy access to alcohol and high levels of drinking can increase the risk of violence against women.

religion. An Amnesty report in 2005 showed that in Europe, North America and Australia more than half of women with disabilities experienced physical abuse, compared to one-third of non-disabled women. In India, women from a lower caste will experience high rates of sexual violence committed by men of a higher caste.

The perpetrators

The perpetrators of violence are often known to their victims, although the Internet is increasingly allowing perpetrators to abuse their victims anonymously. Victims often choose not to report incidents of abuse for fear of being shamed by their families or communities, particularly in regions where the law or state fails to protect them. For this reason, perpetrators of violence are rarely held accountable for their acts.

more likely to experience physical or sexual violence. The World Health Organisation in 2005 showed that 15 per cent of women in Japan had experienced physical and/or sexual violence by an intimate partner in their lifetime, whereas in Ethiopia this figure rose to 71 per cent. Other factors can also increase the likelihood of violence, such as women's ethnicity, class, caste, disability, age or

WHO IS AT RISK?

In October 2013, the World Health Organisation (WHO) identified risk factors associated with intimate partner and sexual violence:

'Risk factors for being a perpetrator include low education, exposure to child maltreatment or witnessing violence in the family, harmful use of alcohol, attitudes accepting of violence and gender inequality.

Risk factors for being a victim of intimate partner and sexual violence include low education, witnessing violence between parents, exposure to abuse during childhood and attitudes accepting violence and gender inequality.'

GROOMING OF YOUNG GIRLS

On 24 April 2009, two teenagers stumbled out of a Derby flat claiming they had been raped. The flat and their accused rapists, Abid Saddique and Mohammed Liaqat, were already being watched by the police as the pair had previously been spotted driving around Derby enticing teenage girls into their car with offers of alcohol.

NEWS FLASH

Date: 2009
Location: Derby, UK
Perpetrators: 13 men arrested, aged between 26 and 38 (11 stood trial)
Victims: 27 known teenage girls aged between 12 and 18
Type of violence: Grooming and sexual abuse of teenage girls

A gang of sexual predators cruised the streets of Derby in cars to groom and exploit teenage girls.

Wide-scale sexual abuse

The victims' statement eventually led to the unearthing of wide-scale sexual abuse involving 27 teenage girls, the youngest of whom was 12, and 13 men, all but one of Asian descent. Typically, the men would meet the girls on the street, invite them to have a drink, smoke or take drugs, after which they would take them to a park, secluded area, guest house or rented house and force them to have sex.

The rapes were often violent, sometimes involving five or six men who would video the attacks on their phones.

> ## 'I was personally shocked at the scale of the abuse we uncovered. It hadn't been reported and it was happening under the radar.'

Detective Superintendent Debbie Platt, who led the police investigation.

The girls would be threatened if they refused the men's advances, and some were held as prisoners.

Saddique was jailed for at least 11 years and Liaqat for a minimum of eight. A further seven of the 13 arrested men were convicted of various offences and sentenced to between 18 months and seven-and-a-half years in jail.

Judge Philip Head told Saddique: he had embarked on a 'reign of terror on girls in Derby.'

Victims are groomed not only by strangers or anonymous sexual predators. In 2014, TV personality Rolf Harris was convicted of several sex offences and had groomed his daughter's best friend from the time she was just 13 years old.

VULNERABLE GIRLS

The young girls in Derby were systematically groomed by their attackers. One 16-year-old victim said: 'They'd take you out, buy you ice creams, take you out for a lovely meal' and they often targeted vulnerable girls from care homes or who were already known to social services. 'They actually take advantage of the fact that no one does care about you really.'

HOW COMMON IS GROOMING?

What led to the sexual grooming of young girls in Derby? Who were the perpetrators and was there a racial element to the abuse? How widespread is sexual grooming and why do some victims fail to report the abuse?

Vulnerable girls

In Derby, the attackers went for young, vulnerable girls, many of whom were known to social services or under their care. In the UK media, questions were raised over why these young girls were allowed out at night and whether they had been adequately protected by the authorities.

As eight of the nine men convicted in Derby were Pakistani Asian, while their victims were white British girls, a heated media debate ensued about whether a significant number of on-street groomers

GROOMING

Often the victims of sexual grooming do not see themselves as victims. When questioned by the police they see their abusers as 'boyfriends' as they are often subtle in their ways, using peer pressure, confusion and emotional blackmail as well as alcohol and drugs.

Teenagers hang out together often drinking and smoking. Peer pressure from within gangs, can lead to abuse from apparent 'friends'.

in the UK were Asian. *The Times* proclaimed there had been a 'conspiracy of silence' over the issue, with people fearful of appearing racist. A 2011 study by CEOP (Child Exploitation and Online Protection agency) suggested that lone offenders tended to be white British males, whereas it seemed that a large proportion of offenders working in groups or gangs were Asian Pakistani men (83 per cent of 52 suspects charged). Others warned about focusing on ethnicity as an issue, saying that the figures were taken from too small a sample of cases. In fact, the main danger to children comes from sexual grooming and exploitation carried out online.

At the launch of I-KIZ, the German version of CEOP, Peter Davies, head of CEOP, stressed to Internet companies that they had to take responsibility for ensuring that children can safeguard themselves when using the Internet.

EXPLOITATION

As access to the Internet increases, so does the exploitation of children online. The term of 'grooming', the initial contact between abuser and victim and its outcome, can be much shorter online. Cases include children being forced to perform sexual acts on webcam by sex abusers, who often pretend to be a child online, and then threaten to show their pictures to friends and family. In September 2013, CEOP reported that in the previous two years 424 children in the UK had been victims of online sexual blackmail. In 2012, CEOP reported that 80 per cent of reported victims of online child sexual exploitation were females.

Peter Davis, head of the British Child Exploitation and Online Protection Centre (CEOP), speaking at the launch of the new Centre for Child Protection on the Internet (I-KIZ) in Berlin, Germany, September 2012.

BEHIND CLOSED DOORS

Violence against women, as reported in our newspapers and other media, represents just the tip of the iceberg when it comes to the true nature and scale of the abuse. Most women are forced to suffer in silence with little hope of escaping their situation, the violence they experience remaining hidden behind closed doors.

Why is it hidden?

Various factors, including shame and fear of retaliation, contribute to women's reluctance to report abuse, particularly if it occurs within the home. Legal and criminal systems in many countries also make the process difficult. Some families and societies view violence within the home or family as normal behaviour and women are conditioned to accept it.

Women who marry young are more likely to believe that it is acceptable for a husband to beat his wife, and lack of economic resources can make it difficult for women to extricate themselves from a violent relationship. Added to that, authorities such as social services or the police often fail to find evidence of violence or to convict its perpetrators.

A classic case of behind closed doors

Former American football player and actor O J Simpson stood trial for the murder of his wife, Nicole Brown, in 1995 but, according to Brown's diaries, she had suffered from violence at his hands since 1985.

violence is that of Mick Philpott in Derby, UK. Philpott had exercised physical and psychological abuse towards women over many years. His house was home to a wife, a mistress and 11 children. All wages and benefits earned by the women were paid into a bank account that he controlled. Neither of them was allowed her own front door keys. The mistress eventually left, taking her children with her. Philpott set fire to his house while his other children slept, making it look as if his mistress was responsible. He and his wife were jailed for the deaths of their children.

Trafficking

Even extreme violence in the form of murder and the disappearance of women can go unnoticed. Trafficking for the purposes of forced labour or sexual slavery, is cleverly hidden from the authorities and once women are caught up in the world of prostitution, there is often no way out.

Female migrant workers can be subject to abuse by their employers, ending up as virtual slaves without anyone in the outside world knowing a thing about it.

'Violence against women is a hidden epidemic, and hidden is a very important word. We all know that women are getting raped as a weapon of war in places like the Democratic Republic of Congo, but in the developed world the problem is hidden.'

Ann Veneman, the former Executive Director of UNICEF.

MISSING WOMEN IN MEXICO

All around Ciudad Juárez, a city on the border with the USA, photographs of missing women are posted on lampposts, walls and shop fronts. Since 1993, hundreds of women have disappeared from the region, many of them raped, tortured and murdered and left in the desert that surrounds the city.

NEWS FLASH

Date: Since 1993
Location: Ciudad Juárez, Mexico
Perpetrator: Vast majority unknown
Victims: According to Amnesty International, more than 370 murdered, and many more have disappeared.
Type of violence: Murder, sexual violence and trafficking

These crosses were erected in Lomas del Poleo Planta Alta, Ciudad Juárez, where the bodies of eight of the women were found in 1996.

Ciudad Juárez

Various factors have been attributed to the murders. Ciudad Juárez is a known location for drug trafficking, with brutal wars between gangs and drug cartels fuelling lawlessness. The city also houses numerous factories, many of whose workers are women who have travelled from poor rural areas and who are vulnerable to exploitation. The growth in the factories in the last 20 years has also coincided with a growth in violence against women.

'Machista' or male-chauvinist culture is

Relatives of women murdered in Ciudad Juárez demonstrated outside the District Attorney's office in July 2007 because of the numbers of crimes against women in the city.

rights organisations as well as accusations of irregularities in state investigations.

also particularly pronounced in the factories and Ciudad Juárez has the highest levels of domestic violence in the country.

The local authorities and police have done little to investigate the disappearances or to convict perpetrators, leading to heavy criticism from human

'No longer of use'

Finally, in June 2013, the state arrested ten men and two women in connection with skeletal remains of girls found near the city. The suspects forced women into prostitution and drug dealing, then killed them when they were 'no longer of use.'

> ## 'The authorities have not the slightest interest in finding our daughters. Everybody's scared to speak up.'
>
> Olga Esparza, mother of an 18-year-old student who disappeared in 2009 after failing to return home from a university course.

WHAT IS HUMAN TRAFFICKING?

Why is it that authorities fail to spot extreme cases of violence against women, such as murders, female trafficking and prostitution? What is female trafficking exactly? And why aren't more perpetrators convicted?

HUMAN TRAFFICKING

The United Kingdom Human Trafficking Centre found 1,186 people who may have been victims of forced labour and trafficking in 2012. The UK media identified 263 victims of forced labour and human trafficking. Sex is the most commonly reported aspect of these crimes, with domestic servitude making up fewer than 3 per cent of victims identified. These domestic 'slaves', however, make up as much as a sixth of the 770 cases of adult exploitation recorded in official statistics.

Child slave workers are common in India. In spite of a government ban, children are still sold by their parents to earn extra money.

Against their will

Human trafficking is the trade in people, most commonly for the purposes of forced labour and sexual slavery. People are held against their will – perhaps in a brothel or as a domestic employee – and forced to provide services for their trafficker or others. It is difficult to know how many people are trafficked worldwide, but the UN estimated that in

2011 as many as 2.5 million people were trafficked, 80 per cent of them women or girls.

While victims of human trafficking can come from any ethnic or social background, they often tend to be in a vulnerable situation, far away from home and in desperate need of money. In some Asian countries, where trafficking has reached alarming figures, prostitutes are unable to complain to police as they will simply be arrested and sent back to their employers.

Women trafficked as domestic servants can suffer beatings and sexual assault. Their passports are withheld, giving them no chance of fleeing home. These women are hidden in their workplace, too frightened to speak out, returning to their own countries if they can rather than alerting authorities of their abuse.

Soroptimist International, a global movement working to improve the lives of women, held a protest rally against human trafficking in Belfast, Northern Ireland, in October 2012. Their work rescues around 1,000 people in the UK each year.

'Eventually I arrived in a bar in Kosovo, [and was] locked inside and forced into prostitution. In the bar I was never paid, I could not go out by myself, the owner became more and more violent as the weeks went by; he was beating me and raping me and the other girls.'

21-year-old Moldovan woman.

EXTREME OPPRESSION

Violence against women occurs in every culture around the world. In some countries, sexual assault by a husband on a wife is not considered a crime – today, in more than 50 countries around the world, marital rape is not seen as an offence. Some cultures condone violence against women and deny women certain rights.

'Three million of the world's women are subjected to FGM every year with 10 per cent dying as a result.'

The Independent newspaper website.

This road sign near Kapchorwa, Uganda, is part of a worldwide campaign to raise awareness of the harm that results from FGM.

Genital mutilation

Female genital mutilation (FGM) is the removal of all or part of the external female genitalia. Around 140 million girls and women worldwide are living with the consequences of FGM. It is most common in Africa and some parts of Asia and Middle East.

It is mostly carried out on young girls between infancy and 15 and is considered by some cultures a necessary part of raising a girl properly. In its most severe form, a woman or girl has the whole of her genitalia removed, and is left with a small opening for intercourse and menstruation. There are no medical benefits, and the procedure commonly leads to infection, sterility, complications with childbirth, newborn deaths, psychological problems and the death of the victim.

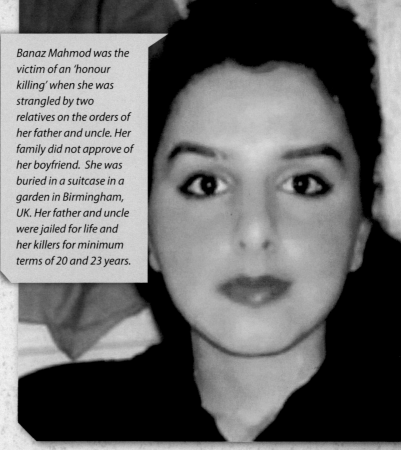

Banaz Mahmod was the victim of an 'honour killing' when she was strangled by two relatives on the orders of her father and uncle. Her family did not approve of her boyfriend. She was buried in a suitcase in a garden in Birmingham, UK. Her father and uncle were jailed for life and her killers for minimum terms of 20 and 23 years.

Honour killings

In some societies women are seen to represent the 'honour' of a family. If they are suspected of sexual infidelity, or even if they have been raped, they can be subjected to violence, in the form of public stoning and murder (known as 'honour killings'). Disputes over dowries or when a woman turns down a suitor – even if she doesn't get along with her husband's family – can also lead to violence. This has involved acid burning (where acid is thrown at the victim), murder by the woman's in-laws or even by her own family.

Forced Marriage outlawed in UK

A forced marriage is where one or both people do not (or in cases of people with learning disabilities, cannot) consent to a marriage and pressure or abuse is used to make them comply. A new law came into force in 2014 in England and Wales that makes it a criminal offence to force anyone into marriage.

'I have met some of the victims. They speak about wedlock being used as a weapon and the horrors to which this can lead, such as rape, abuse and unwanted pregnancy.'

Sayeeda Warsi, *The Guardian*, 2011.

SHOOTING OF A SCHOOL GIRL

On the afternoon of 9 October 2012, a Taliban gunman boarded a bus taking children home from school in Mingora, Pakistan. One of the schoolgirls was 14-year-old Malala Yousafzai. The gunman deliberately shot the defenceless girl in the head and neck.

NEWS FLASH

Date: 9 October 2012
Location: Mingora in Swat Valley, northwest Pakistan
Perpetrators: The Taliban
Victim: 14-year-old Malala Yousafzai
Type of violence: Attempted murder by shooting

Malala Yousafzai was flown to the UK for surgery after the shooting and spent many months recovering.

Speaking openly

From the age of 11, Yousafzai had been writing a blog for the BBC about life as a girl under the Taliban. She spoke openly about the need for girls' education, something that the Taliban strongly opposes. The school bus shooting horrified Pakistanis across the political and religious spectrum, many voicing their disgust in the newspapers, on television and through social media, leading to protests in many cities. The assassination attempt also received worldwide media coverage and condemnation.

This grainy image taken by a hidden camera shows Taliban police beating a woman in the street in Afghanistan.

THE TALIBAN

The Taliban took over the Swat Valley in Pakistan in 2007. The Pakistani Government regained control of the region in 2009, but could never fully stabilise the area, which continues to suffer from violence and intimidation. The Taliban, Islamic fundamentalists who had formed a government in Afghanistan between 1996 and 2001, are condemned internationally for their brutal treatment of women. Under their rule, women were forbidden an education, had to be accompanied by a male relative outside the home and were required to wear a burqa (a garment that covers the head and body). Those who disobeyed were severely disciplined or beaten.

Yousafzai survived the attack and now lives and goes to school in Birmingham, UK. She regularly speaks about her firm belief in education for all children, she has written a memoir and she was nominated for a Nobel Peace Prize in 2013. A UN petition launched under her name 'I am Malala' has led to the ratification of Pakistan's first Right to Education Bill. The Taliban stands by its decision to target her for criticising Islam and in 2013 said they will try again to kill her.

'She was attacked and shot by extremists who don't want girls to have an education and don't want girls to speak for themselves, and don't want girls to become leaders,'

US Secretary of State Hillary Clinton.

SHOULD OTHERS INTERFERE?

Do countries have the right to interfere in another country's cultural practices and treatment of women? While we may condemn extreme oppression (such as the Taliban's treatment of women), should Westerners be more careful when considering such practices as arranged marriages or women's head coverings?

Symbol of oppression?

The West often decries the Muslim tradition of women wearing head coverings as a symbol of oppression, whereas to many Muslims it is seen as liberating and spiritually cleansing.

Covering all but the face and hands in public is deemed a suitably modest form of dress. Some Muslims believe that even those should be covered. Is our condemnation a form of Islamophobia and discrimination?

HEAD COVERINGS

There are a wide variety of head coverings worn by women in the Muslim world. The hijab is a simple head scarf that covers the hair. In Saudi Arabia, women typically wear a niqab, which is a veil that covers the face, leaving the eyes visible. The chador is a full body cloak that is common in Iran and the khimar covers the shoulders, neck and hair, leaving the face exposed. In Indonesia, head coverings are optional and in Turkey and France, burqas (shown left) are banned in public.

Young Muslim girls start wearing the hijab (head scarf) from puberty, sometimes earlier depending on the family traditions.

Campaigns like Mumsnet's 'Let Girls Be Girls' aim to ease the pressure on young girls to dress and wear make-up like young women.

Is the West any better?

Is the treatment and depiction of women in the West any better? Bombarded by images in the media, women are under pressure to look a certain way and to be sexualised from a young age. Some say that women who wear make-up and high heels are just as oppressed as women who wear a head covering. Violence against women still occurs in the West, with many women and girls becoming victims of sexual harassment, domestic abuse, rape or related psychological problems such as eating disorders.

> '...we worked hard to influence the products that were being sold to our daughters.'
>
> Mumsnet on their 'Let Girls Be Girls' campaign.

DEBATE

Should the wearing of the burqa be banned?

YES

It deprives women of identity and social interaction and is a symbol of oppression and inequality between men and women. It can restrict a woman's vision and movement.

NO

We need to respect Muslim cultural and religious views. Wearing the burqa helps women to fulfil Muslim commandments and be modest. It is no more dangerous and unhealthy for women to wear than high heels.

BODY CONTROL

In many parts of the world, sons are favoured over daughters as it is thought that boys present less of a financial burden on a family. Girls, who are required to pay sizeable dowries to future husbands, are seen as a drain on a family's wealth. As a result, where resources are scarce, daughters might receive less food, medical care and education than their brothers.

Missing girls

This kind of gender discrimination can also result in the abortion of female foetuses and the killing of infant girls, a problem particularly associated with Asia.

Many claim this has led to marked gender imbalances in the populations of some Asian countries, including India, China, Vietnam, South Korea and Singapore. It is also known as the 'missing girls' phenomenon. In 2012, China had 120 boys for every 100 girls and UNICEF

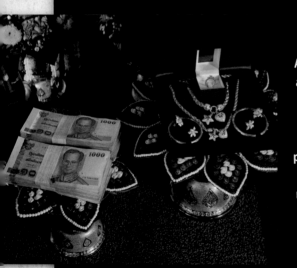

DOWRY

Across south Asia, forced marriages occur regularly and can sometimes be the most demeaning rite of passage a woman endures. For some marriages, the bride's family essentially gives her to the highest bidder, and for others the bride's family pays exorbitant amounts in dowry to the husband's family. Some men, if unhappy with the dowry, might resort to killing their wives, often by setting them on fire. In India, the Ministry of Human Resource Development estimated that there were 5,157 dowry murders in 1991.

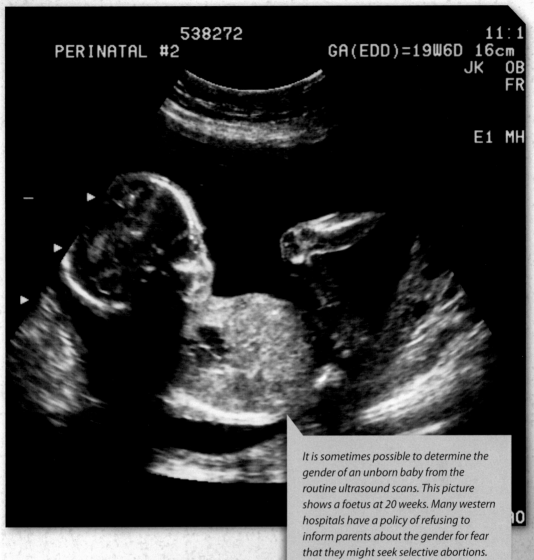

It is sometimes possible to determine the gender of an unborn baby from the routine ultrasound scans. This picture shows a foetus at 20 weeks. Many western hospitals have a policy of refusing to inform parents about the gender for fear that they might seek selective abortions.

estimates that up to 50 million girls are missing from India's population as a result of gender discrimination.

In 2012, the UN estimated that between 33 million and 160 million girls were not alive today because of abortion or infanticide. The problem is particularly acute in China, partly as a result of the country's one-child policy, which leads to female infanticide, sex-selective abortion and forced sterilisation.

'They say bringing up a girl is like watering a neighbour's plant. From birth to death, the expenditure is there.'

R Venkatachalam, director of the Community Services Guild of Madras, India.

FORCED ABORTION

On 11 June 2012, images of 23-year-old Feng Jianmei lying on a hospital bed with the corpse of her aborted daughter next to her spread virally on the Internet. Two days afterwards, more than a million angry comments had been left on Weibo, China's version of Twitter, with many people describing the action as 'murder'.

NEWS FLASH

Date: 2 June 2012
Location: Ankang, Shaanxi province, China
Perpetrators: Local Chinese officials
Victim: 23-year-old Feng Jianmei and her unborn female daughter
Type of violence: Forced abortion

Feng's family caused an outcry when they posted this image of her with the baby (not shown here) on the Internet.

Illegal abortion

Feng Jianmei was seven months pregnant with her second child, when she was forcibly removed from her home by local officials, who took her to hospital where she received an injection on 2 June to abort her baby. The victim and her partner had apparently failed to fill in application forms for the baby, and the couple was unable to pay a fine of 40,000 yuan (around £4,000) set by the officials for violating China's one-child policy.

Local authorities later concluded that Feng had been forced into an illegal

Promoting China's one-child policy, this sculpture in a village in Sichuan Province, central China, depicts the country's idea of the perfect family.

abortion and the city of Ankang issued a formal apology. The township government offered compensation to Feng and her husband, but the family has been unable to pursue any form of legal action.

Organisations around the world, including the European Parliament and US House of Representatives, condemned the treatment of Feng Jianmei and forced abortion in general.

'Feng Jianmei's story demonstrates how the One-Child Policy continues to sanction violence against women every day.'

Chai Ling of NGO All Girls Allowed.

ONE-CHILD POLICY

China's one-child policy was introduced in 1979 to curb population growth. The policy is controversial because of the way it is implemented and its implication in forced abortions and female infanticide, which contribute to China's gender imbalance. Pressure for change to China's one-child policy is mounting and in November 2013, China announced that families can have two children if one parent is an only child.

HOW DOES THE MEDIA ACT?

Graphic images of Feng Jianmei's abortion were published on the Internet and went viral within a matter of hours. How important was social media in her case? How does the media depict the issue of violence against women – does it help expose the plight of victims, generating debate, or does it contribute to the problem?

A force for good

The ensuing outrage and discussion over Feng Jianmei's forced abortion were only made possible by the Internet and power of social media. As this case shows, social media can help to raise awareness and inspire people to engage in social activism.

Modern society depends hugely on the media, in our daily lives we rely on the information we get from the Internet, TV, film and print media. It has the power to influence society in a positive way, bringing important issues to our attention, exposing stories that highlight abuse or

Nigella Lawson, right, and her then husband Charles Saatchi were seen arguing at a London restaurant in June 2013 . He was famously photographed gripping her by the throat, leading to allegations of domestic violence.

exploitation, generating debate and change. The media is an important tool, used by governments and organisations working for women such as the Half The Sky Movement which tackles the oppression of women globally through books, celebrity endorsements, television programmes, Internet sites, Facebook and all forms of social media.

A destructive power

While the media can be a force for good, it can also influence in the most destructive ways, contributing to and justifying violence against women. Images of submissive, objectified and victimised women are often seen in advertisements, on TV, film and the Internet. Pornography – which makes up 12 per cent of all websites – commonly presents even more extreme examples of violence, where female subordination and rape are common themes, where violence

against women is seen as acceptable, if not the norm.

Can we also trust the news reports we see covering issues and stories of violence against women? Does it tend to sensationalise stories, or ignore the more mundane examples of violence, such as domestic abuse?

A highly sexualised advertising poster in China's New World shopping mall in Beijing depicts Hong Kong actress Charmaine Sheh promoting Perfect Shape beauty products.

'Even three years ago, Ms Feng's suffering might have gone unnoticed... but her relatives uploaded the graphic pictures onto the Internet, and soon microblogs had flashed them to millions of people across the country.'

The Economist, 23 June 2012.

WEAPON OF WAR

Violence against women, in the form of rape, mutilation and forced sexual slavery, has long been used as a tactic of war. It can be isolated, opportunistic or part of a wider battle or brutal massacre. Sometimes, it is even actively encouraged by military leaders who use it as a deliberate tactic.

Psychological warfare

Violence against women can be used to inflict terror on the population at large, as a form of psychological warfare to humiliate an enemy and shatter communities. The systematic rape of women in Bosnia in the 1990s, the estimated 200,000 women raped during the battle for Bangladeshi independence in 1971, and countless other examples from the past century all bear witness to this.

War crime

For a long time it was simply accepted that violence against women was inevitable during times of conflict and few efforts

US soldiers regularly conducted house-to-house searches in Iraq, looking for terrorists but also for anyone being held captive. Here they prepare for a search in Ramadi, central Iraq, in 2005.

Hundreds of Congolese women, victims of sexual violence, have taken refuge in the village of Buganga – known as the village of victims. Mama Masika (in the centre), once a victim herself, helps them start a new life there.

were made to prosecute perpetrators. Since 1946, the Geneva Convention has, in theory, protected people from rape and violence in conflict zones. In 1998, the UN passed a resolution classing sexual violence in conflict, including rape, as a war crime.

On 24 September 2013, 113 countries endorsed a UN Declaration of Commitment to end Sexual Violence in Conflict in an attempt to raise awareness of the crimes, and respond to and reduce sexual violence in conflict zones.

> **'In Bosnia, systematic rape was used as part of the strategy of ethnic cleansing... Women were raped so they could give birth to a Serbian baby.'**
>
> **Médicins Sans Frontières.**

CONFLICT ZONES

- In the Democratic Republic of Congo, approximately 1,100 rapes are being reported each month, with an average of 36 women and girls raped every day. It is believed that over 200,000 women have suffered from sexual violence in that country since armed conflict began.
- The rape and sexual violation of women and girls is pervasive in the conflict in the Darfur region of Sudan.
- Between 250,000 and 500,000 women were raped during the 1994 genocide in Rwanda.
- Sexual violence was a characterising feature of the 14-year-long civil war in Liberia.

MASS RAPE OF WOMEN

One of the most deadly wars in Africa began in 1998 in the Democratic Republic of the Congo. Since its outbreak, five million people have lost their lives and at least 200,000 women have been raped by the Congolese army, militias, local gangs and other civilians.

NEWS FLASH

Date: 1998 onwards
Location: Democratic Republic of the Congo (DR Congo), Central Africa
Perpetrators: Congolese Army, local militias and gangs
Victim: Estimated 200,000 women and girls (men and boys also raped)
Type of violence: Rape and torture

This woman is one of the thousands who have been used as so-called 'weapons of war' in the DR Congo.

A dangerous place

Although the war officially ended in 2003, fighting has carried on in the east of the country, and some reports claim that the number of rapes is far higher, with 400,000 rapes in just one year from 2006–07 according to the *American Journal of Public Health*.

The types of violence inflicted on civilians, young and old, include rape, forced prostitution and sexual slavery, torture, genital mutilation and shooting. Reports tell of soldiers entering villages

These Congolese soldiers are attending a seven-month training programme in field sanitation, gender-based violence and military professionalism in DR Congo in 2010 as part of an operation led by US Africa Command.

and towns and conducting mass rapes with extreme brutality, many ordered to rape by their superior officers. The rape of men is also prevalent. Many of the rape victims are adolescent girls, with some reports claiming that 10 per cent of victims are children under the age of ten.

Some efforts have been made to prevent the atrocities, with the UN putting pressure on Congolese army generals to prosecute soldiers accused of sexual violence. Several military leaders have been charged with sexual violence by the International Criminal Court and in November 2013, after months of international pressure, 39 soldiers were put on trial in the eastern Congo. In general, however, human rights organisations point out that the Congolese government has done little to prosecute the perpetrators or provide adequate help for the rape victims.

'I was just coming back from the river to fetch water... Two soldiers came up to me and told me that if I refuse to sleep with them, they will kill me. They beat me and ripped my clothes. One of the soldiers raped me...'

15-year-old girl, Minova, South Kivu, Human Rights Watch.

WHAT ARE THE EFFECTS?

What effect does war rape have on women and their communities? How does sexual violence in general affect its victims, the global health and our economy? Is it a worldwide epidemic?

During conflict

The effects of rape and sexual violence during conflict are far-reaching. Medical repercussions can include broken limbs, pregnancy, transmission of sexual disease (20 per cent of women who have been attacked are HIV positive), severe internal injury, infertility, incontinence and death. Psychologically, victims can suffer from post-traumatic stress, depression and even attempted suicide. Rape victims can also be isolated by their families and communities, abandoned by husbands, and, in extreme cases, murdered in the belief that they have brought shame to their family and community.

Global consequences

Victims of sexual violence, in whatever form, suffer from a huge range of physical and psychological problems, which often restrict their ability to participate in public life. It also causes extensive suffering and negative health consequences for a

THE EFFECTS OF RAPE

• Victims of non-partner attacks are 2.6 times more likely to experience depression and anxiety compared with women who have not experienced violence.
• Those abused by their partners are almost twice as likely to have similar problems.
• Victims are more likely to have alcohol problems, abortions and acquire sexually transmitted diseases and HIV.

This Allied army officer in Rangoon, Burma (Myanmar), in August 1945 is talking to a young ethnic Chinese woman who had been abused in one of the Japanese army's 'comfort battalions' – official military brothels.

to justice, as well as the indirect costs of lost employment are more than you would think. A 2009 report in the UK estimated the direct and indirect cost of domestic violence to be £16 billion per year.

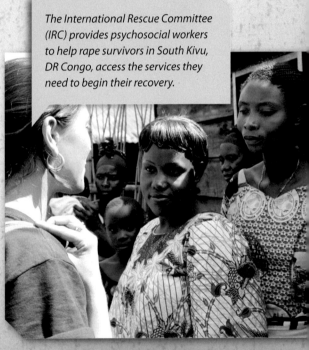

The International Rescue Committee (IRC) provides psychosocial workers to help rape survivors in South Kivu, DR Congo, access the services they need to begin their recovery.

significant proportion of women in the world. A 2013 World Health Organisation report indicated that around a third of all women worldwide experience some form of sexual violence. In many countries the figure is significantly higher.

Financial cost?

The human pain and suffering inflicted on victims of sexual violence is extensive and almost impossible to quantify. Is there a financial cost? Costs involved in treating women and children, bringing perpetrators

'Worldwide, it has been estimated that violence against women is as serious a cause of death and incapacity among women of reproductive age as cancer, and a greater cause of ill-health than traffic accidents and malaria combined.'

World Health Organisation website.

CHALLENGING VIOLENCE

What are people doing to challenge and end violence against women? What can we all do to bring about the changes that are needed to free women from the fear of violent abuse and the consequences of such attacks – or is this just a problem for women to solve?

Men and boys

Everyone should speak out against violence against women and men and boys have a crucial role to play. They can teach others to embrace equality between the sexes, raise awareness about the consequences of violence against women, support the victims of violence and provide a positive role model for other men and boys.

A wave of protest

Over recent years, many women have

practice
MAKES PERFECT
WALKAMILETORONTO.COM

walk a mile in her shoes.®
AN INTERNATIONAL WALK TO END VIOLENCE AGAINST WOMEN

The 'Walk a Mile in Her Shoes' campaign aims to raise men's awareness about the serious causes and effects of violence against women. This event in Toronto, Canada, in 2013 attracted more than 400 participants.

Men and women in New Dehli, India, gathered on 5 March 2013 to protest against the rising number of rape incidents in the city.

protested, angered by incidences of extreme violence against women. During Egypt's political uprisings between 2011 and 2013, mob-led attacks on women as well as the subsequent beating of female protestors by the Egyptian military led thousands of women to march in protest through the streets of Cairo. The rape of a Delhi student in 2012 (see pages 40–41) led to rallies and marches across south Asia, many of the protests centering on the authorities' failure to prevent and prosecute men involved in violent attacks.

ONE BILLION RISING

The One Billion Rising campaign, launched by American playwright Eve Ensler in 2013 held rallies in more than 190 countries across the world on February 12 (see page 5). Protests ranged from the first ever flashmob in Mogadishu in Somalia to 13,000 women forming human chains in Bangladesh's cities. The 'one billion' refers to the statistic that one in three women will be raped or beaten in their lifetime, or about a billion worldwide.

ONE BILLION RISING

'Men must teach each other that real men do not violate or oppress women – and that a woman's place is not just in the home or the field, but in schools and offices and boardrooms.'

UN Secretary-General Ban Ki-Moon.

GANG RAPE IN DELHI

At about 9.30 pm on 16 December 2012, a 23-year-old student and a male friend boarded an off-duty charter bus in south Delhi. On the bus were six men who proceeded to beat the male unconscious, then drag the woman to the back of the bus where she was beaten and raped while the bus drove around Delhi.

NEWS FLASH

Date: 16 December 2012
Location: Munirka, New Delhi, India
Perpetrators: Six men, including a 17-year-old juvenile
Victim: 23-year-old Jyoti Singh Pandey
Type of violence: Beaten and gang raped, with extreme brutality

To comply with Indian law, the victim's name was not released to the media. Her father later released her name as Jyoti Singh Pandey in the hope that it would help other victims come forward.

The outcome

The attackers used an iron rod in their assault on the victim, who suffered horrific injuries as a result. After several attempts by surgeons to save her life, she died on the 29 December.

The following year, all six attackers were arrested and tried, with four of the perpetrators sentenced to death by hanging on 13 September. One of the men died in custody before the trial and the other attacker, a 17-year-old, was given the maximum sentence for a juvenile of three years.

Outpouring of anger

The incident unleashed an unprecedented outpouring of anger and grief in India. Within days of the attack, thousands of people took to the streets throughout the country, with further protests in Bangladesh, Nepal, Sri Lanka and Pakistan, all calling for an end to sexual violence, an overhaul of attitudes to women and legal reform.

The Indian and international media gave the incident unprecedented coverage, and organisations, including the UN, demanded that the Indian government take up radical reforms and make women's lives safer. The Indian government has responded with amendments to the law, the introduction of fast-track courts as well as improvements in police procedure. As a consequence, more women are reporting rapes in India, but many still struggle to find justice.

Dehli police escort two of the gang rapists, Mukesh Singh (far left) and Vinay Sharma (right), to the High Court in New Delhi, on 24 September 2013 for their death sentences to be confirmed.

EVE TEASING

In India, sexual harassment on public transport is common, the media often dubbing it as 'eve teasing'. Indian activists have repeatedly argued that this contributes to the widespread acceptance of sexual harassment in public places.

WHO WAS TO BLAME?

Lawyers defending the rapists in Delhi pointed some of the blame at the victim, claiming she should not have been out at night, and that they had never heard of a 'respected lady' being raped in India. Was the victim in any way to blame and how does this compare to incidents in the West? How has the media treated the case?

Indian women in Parmandapur, a rural area of Uttar Pradesh, participate in an awareness course on sexual violence.

Rape culture

The media coverage of the rape in Delhi highlighted the plight of women in India who suffer from harassment and discrimination throughout their lives, inequality that, some say, fuels a 'rape culture' in India. The widespread coverage prompted open debate about the issue of violence against women, bringing it to the forefront of the national agenda. Social media also played an important part in mobilising support, with people voicing their anger through Twitter, Facebook and other social media.

> '**Sexual violence is no stranger to Indian society. What is new, is the way in which cases like those I've mentioned, are being picked up by the press and talked about around the family dining table. Before the turmoil of the Delhi rape, the weight of 'sharam' or shame that surrounded the sexual violation of women prevented most from reporting attacks even to their families.**'

Anita Anand, *The Telegraph*, 11 September 2013.

In the West

Some critics have maintained that the media's coverage in the West demonised Indian society, while ignoring the enormity of Western rape culture. *The Wall Street Journal* gave the statistics that in India just over a quarter of alleged rapes result in a conviction. However, in the US only 24 per cent of alleged rapes result in arrest. Similarly, the BBC stated that a woman is raped in Delhi every 14 hours, equating to 625 victims a year. In England and Wales, with a population about 3.5 times the size of Delhi, the number of recorded rapes of women is far higher – 9,509 a year.

Women gather in London in March 2014 to support Million Women Rise, an annual event held to raise awareness about violence against women.

TAKING ACTION AGAINST VIOLENCE

So what can we do to end violence against women?
How can we change attitudes where women are treated as
inferior, where violence is protected by cultural practices,
hidden behind closed doors and deemed acceptable?

Learn about violence

Taking time to learn about violence against women, in all its various forms, is an important first step. It will help you to recognise violence if it happens to you or to someone you know, or if you read about victims of abuse and violence in the news.

Positions of power

Passing laws that criminalise violence against women is another important way to redefine limits of acceptable behaviour towards women. It can help to prevent violence, protect victims and punish assailants. But passing laws is not enough as laws have to be implemented and enforced. More importantly, cultural attitudes towards women have to be changed, and this process takes much longer and needs to involve every level of society.

Organisations like womensaid.org.uk offer help and advice for victims of violence or friends who want to lend their support.

#TIMETOACT

#TIMETOACT   #TIMETOACT   #TIMETOACT

London's End Sexual Violence in Conflict conference, hosted by Angelina Jolie and former British Foreign Secretary William Hague, was attended by around 1,700 delegates from 129 countries (see page 6). The summit agreed steps to tackle the use of rape as a weapon of war.

People in government and positions of power can help to change the trends of culture from the top down, but people from all walks of life need to recognise violence when they see it, voice their opposition to it and demand change. Communities need to bring violence against women and girls, hidden and protected by tradition or cultural practice, out from behind closed doors, and collectively refuse to accept it as normal behaviour. Women need to be viewed by men and boys as equal partners and as valued, respected members of our communities.

What can you do?

Learn about the various types of violence that happen in your own community and across the world. Talk about it at home, at school and with your friends and family. Join in with global campaigns like One Billion Rising, recognise and flag up examples of sexism in the media and consider all angles when reading about violence against women in the news.

'Violence against women is always a violation of human rights; it is always a crime; and it is always unacceptable. Let us take this issue with the deadly seriousness that it deserves.

UN Secretary-General Ban Ki-Moon.

GLOSSARY

abortion
An operation or other medical procedure to terminate a pregnancy and prevent the child being born alive.

anxiety
A state of intense worry or distress, causing physical symptoms such as headaches and stomach problems.

assailant
Someone who attacks another person.

atrocities
Acts of extreme violence or cruelty most usually associated with the military in war zones or terrorist activities.

caste
A social group limited to those of the same social standing or class.

chauvinist
A man (male chauvinist) who believes that men are superior to women.

consequence
Something that happens as a result of actions that have already occurred.

constitutive
An important part of any thing that plays a major role in establishing that thing or in making it happen.

depression
A sad mood that badly affects a person's thoughts, feelings, actions and attitude towards others.

discrimination
Unfair or unusual treatment of someone, perhaps because of their race, colour, age or sex.

domestic
Something that happens in or belongs in your home or in your home country.

dowry
Property or money that is given by her parents to a daughter when she marries and then belongs to her new family.

economic
Relating to the economics or financial situation of a family or community.

ethnicity
Belonging to a certain race, national, social or otherwise 'ethnic' group.

gender
A person's sexual type – male or female.

genocide
The murder of a large number of people, especially those of a particular race, nationality or social group.

grooming

The tactic used by paedophiles or other sexual predators to gain the trust of their victims and prepare them to be subjected to sexual abuse.

harassment

Aggressive pestering that intimidates victims, putting them under pressure.

HIV

Human Immunodeficiency Virus – the virus that causes AIDS. Those who are HIV positive are infected with the virus.

infanticide

The murder of an infant, particularly a baby under the age of 1 year.

media

The channels used for communicating news or other information. They include newspapers, books, television and radio, as well as the Internet and social media, such as Twitter or Facebook.

migrant

A person who moves from one place to another, especially when looking for work.

militia

A fighting force made up of citizen volunteers or non-professional soldiers.

objectified

When someone is treated in a degrading way as though they are an object rather than a human being.

oppression

Cruel, harsh or unfair treatment that causes the victim distress.

overt

Open, in plain sight, not hidden in any way.

perpetrator

A person who deliberately does something harmful or illegal.

pornography

Writing or images that describe or show sex acts.

prostitution

Participating in sex acts for payment.

psychological

Can describe anything affecting the mind and a person's emotional condition.

rape

Forcing another person to have sex against his or her will.

sexually transmitted disease

Also known as an STD, this covers a range of diseases passed from one person to another when participating in sex acts.

sterilisation

An operation or medical procedure that leaves the subject unable to have children.

trafficking

Human trafficking involves transporting people illegally from one place or country to another for profit.

unprecedented

Something without precedent, meaning that it has never happened before.

war crimes

Crimes that are against the accepted rules of war, including genocide and the use of banned weapons.

INDEX